IN THE EMBRACE OF FEAR

Books by the same author

Cyclones of the Human Heart
The Shadow of Rainbow
The Children of Signatures
The African in the Mirror
The Days of Illusions
Fouta Celebrates Life

IN THE EMBRACE OF FEAR

Fear as a determinant factor of Under-development in Sub-Sahara Africa

Development = 1/Exploitation X Fear^2

Abimbola Lagunju

iUniverse, Inc.

New York Lincoln Shanghai

In The Embrace of Fear

Fear as a determinant factor of Under-development in Sub-Sahara Africa

iUniverse books may be ordered through booksellers or by contacting:

iUniverse
2021 Pine Lake Road, Suite 100
Lincoln, NE 68512
www.iuniverse.com
1-800-Authors (1-800-288-4677)

Front Cover Picture: Abimbola Lagunju

ISBN-13: 978-0-595-41370-6 (pbk)
ISBN-13: 978-0-595-85719-7 (ebk)
ISBN-10: 0-595-41370-6 (pbk)
ISBN-10: 0-595-85719-1 (ebk)

Printed in the United States of America

For Veronique and Gerard Xavier

Contents

Acknowledgements

It is not only Black Africans who harbour concerns for the future of the continent. I have discovered in the course of many discussions and interactions that many people from diverse cultures are embarrassed by the history of Africa, worried about its present condition, and deeply concerned for its future.

I will like to thank Ignacio Packer and Mario Gehri for nurturing an optimistic vision for Africa, and Marie Jeanne Hautbois for her unflagging commitment to a difficult part of the continent, in spite of enormous odds. My gratitude also goes to all others who, at on time or the other have shared their non-conceited views with me.

I am grateful to Louis Camara, my friend and mentor, for keeping the literary lamp burning; and to Marc Weil for his friendship and support.

They do not necessarily share the views expressed in this book.

Abimbola Lagunju

Introduction

At no time in human history has the world witnessed such an explosive and rapidly advancing human and societal development as has been recorded in the last fifty years. Those societies that for various reasons have had a head start are unrelentingly devising ways and means not only to keep themselves far ahead of the pack, but also to meet the challenges that the changing landscape of our universe will pose in years to come. Survival can no longer be taken as a given. A society must struggle for it. This struggle entails concerted efforts to move away from basic existence to qualitative life. Manacling mental attitudes that inhibit this process put a society at peril. Fear, the most frightening mental attitude erodes self-confidence and blurs vision when given a free rein. Any society caught in the clutches of fear gradually wastes away.

For centuries, Africa has lived with fear and adapted itself to its vagaries. The challenges of the modern world have not only made this approach obsolete but very dangerous. Africa needs to rise up from its slumber in order to save itself. In the words of Lenrie Peters, "between Alpha and Omega is now; this is the lost time and future time".

"..oh continent of great hopes
and boundless possibilities
will the seed grain perish forever?[1]"

This essay is inspired by my observations and analysis of the environment in which I live. It has no other source but my concerns for Sub-Sahara Africa and its future. I can only hope that the analysis is wrong, and that my *fear* for the future is unfounded.

Dakar, August 31, 2006.

FEAR

Fear, a natural self-preservation human reaction, transforms into a most debilitating and destructive emotion when left unchecked. It seeks to self-multiply and to dominate its victim. The victim becomes a hostage to real and unreal terror-inducing situations, objects, or conditions. The relationship between fear (whether real or unreal) and its victim is characterised by a constant energy interplay within a closed system between the two. Within this system, fear exerts a powerful negative energy field, which tends to pull the victim into the abyss of its nucleus. In order to survive, the victim must be resourceful. This resourcefulness demands tremendous amount of mental energy, focus, and vision. Fear, being a natural phenomenon does not disappear; the onus is on the victim to put its negative field in check in order to guarantee his survival qualitatively. The more resourceful the victim is, the more the quality he adds to his existence. The less resourceful the victim is, the more the influence (with all the attending consequences) of fear, and the victim simply exists as an entity occupying a given space in a given time until fear overwhelms him.

When locked in the closed energy system with fear, the need for self-preservation invokes two types of reaction in the victim—fight or flight as is commonly known. In the first case, the victim seeks to dominate at all costs. He expends great amount of energy in order to shift the energy balance between it and fear in his favour. The victim seeks to dominate the cause of his fears. He may succeed if the cause of fear is real. If however, the fear-inducing situation or condition is unreal, the victim, faced with the failure of his aggressive approach will seek to convert his illusions into reality. In the bid to prove his sanity and in order to avoid ridicule, he strives to convert his imagined fears into real fears through conscious self-delusion and manipulation of others. In most cases, this strategy is successful because of the infectious nature of fear. The elemental pack instinct soon dominates any form of rational thought process and those in the pack that knew that the original fear-inducing situation was imaginary soon begin to see it as real. Under this situation, truth loses its universal meaning and essence, and distortion of facts becomes the norm. In this state of mind, the aggressive victim of fear invents events that did not happen, distorts events that happened and remembers events that never took place.

In the second case, the victim of fear does not seek to dominate it. He concedes grounds to fear and creates defensive mechanisms to self-protect. His morbid obsession for self-preservation is however not directed at overcoming the fear-inducing factors or situations, rather it is directed at creating cowering mechanisms that further embolden fear. Fear draws its strength from this morbid obsession of its victim to survive at all costs, even in the most precarious of conditions. The continuous shift of energy balance in favour of fear gradually depletes its victims and incapacitates him physically and emotionally. The victim becomes fixated only on his existence as an entity occupying a particular space in a given time. This obsession for mere survival does not leave any energy or time for the victim to seek to improve the quality of his life.

Fear in individuals has been well studied, documented and can be treated. Under professional guidance, individuals suffering from irrational fears learn to confront the fear-inducing factors or situations as part of their therapy. In the course of their treatment, they learn to shift the energy balance in their favour, thereby replenishing their depleted reserves. This replenishment manifests in increased productivity of the individual and in some cases, it unleashes hitherto unknown creativity and resourcefulness. The victim, thus liberated from obsession for mere survival seeks to add quality to his existence.

Societies or communities can also suffer from collective fear. However, unlike in the individual, society fear may not be easily diagnosable. It may manifest in different intractable problems and characteristics that define the society and its philosophy of life. Like an individual, a society may harbour fears of the known and the unknown. Society fears may also be real or unreal. Known sources of fear may be founded on the collective historical experience of the society and in many instances, future unreal fears harboured by this society originate from this historical experience. As is the case in an individual, a society may convert unreal and imaginary fears into a real menacing agent through collective self-delusion, manipulation, and disinformation. The fear of the unknown is common to all societies; however, some societies tend to fear the unknown more than the others. This type of fear could be social (based on historical interactions between cultures in which one predated the other) or natural (based on the complexity of nature and the unpredictability of its elements). The fear of the unknown may be real or imaginary; however, it is largely imaginary and a society may expend enormous resources to prove the imminent transformation of these imaginary fears into real life-threatening ones. Imaginary fears of the elements may become real through mathematical deductions. Meticulous calculation of the flight path of a meteor, which may potentially hit the earth, is an example of this. Almost invariably, societies that tend to be aggressive in the face of real fears (fight variant) are the most active in the effort to understand the nature of imaginary unknown fears. They seek to understand and to dominate any form of fear.

Socially motivated unknown fears have their origins in historical interactions between cultures. The victims and perpetrators of historical wrongs and aggression harbour eternal distrust of each other. The victims fear a repeat of the aggression while the perpetrators are wary of revenge by their victims. Fears that evoke this kind of reaction are mostly racial, religious, ethnic, ideological or simply, personal in nature. These fears have their roots in irrational bigotry that ridicules any claims to civilization by humanity.

A society reacts to fear in the same way as individuals, either through fight or through flight. Societies that choose to confront any form of fear under any circumstances have, at one time or the other, successfully confronted and dominated many odds in their history, and have learnt to maintain in their favour, the energy balance between them and fear. These societies put enormous resources—military, financial, and scientific at confronting any form of fear. They become convinced of their invincibility and are most destructive when they perceive a real or imaginary menace. Their conviction in their invincibility very often inhibits the rational thought process, and unbridled violence or the threat of it becomes their communication strategy. They in turn constitute themselves into a source of real fear for other societies.

On the other hand, a society that chooses to cower in the face of fear, directs all is meagre resources, not at dominating fear, but at containing it. In this society, the energy balance is in favour of fear. The society cowers before internal and external, real and unreal fear-inducing factors and directs the little energy that it has to ensuring its existence in the most basic, very often, precarious form. In order to justify this strategy, such a society even expends some of its meagre resources at magnifying fear. It portrays fear as an un-overcome-able adversary. The society adopts self-induced helplessness as a way of life. As the known source of fear evolves, the society fear acquires bigger dimensions. This fear, though *acquired* soon becomes a trait that is passed from generation to generation with increasing magnitude. On the contrary, the energy and the willingness to overcome these odds diminish from generation to generation. The comprehensibility of the nature of these fear-inducing factors, which may facilitate the process of overcoming them, soon becomes muddled up, and living tremulously with, and in fear becomes a way of life. The challenges of ever-changing external and internal environments further complicate the relationship between this society and fear. Fear thus acquires bigger dimension with each new challenge and further pushes the society to the fringes of elementary existence. As is the case with individuals, the absence of energy reserves manifests in a collective under-productivity, absence of vision and lack of resourcefulness. This lack of collective internal drive to harness the little available energy to overcome fear soon translates into intractable debilitating collective illness, "a cultivated case of social schizophrenia"[2] characterised by a fatalistic resignation to what the society conveniently identifies as its "fate". Concern for shallow and mundane issues that inhibit productivity and resourcefulness becomes the principal preoccupation of this society. Life becomes a captive of fear, and the right to it cannot be fully exercised physically, mentally and spiritually. Thus resigned to its "fate", the phobic-society tacitly accepts the superiority of other societies who have overcome fear and have used all resources available to them (including human and material resources from the "fate" society) to develop themselves.

In this prostrate condition, the phobic-society seeks to define its identity within the confines of this "fate". Values are redefined to portray the relationship of the society with fear. Fear induces "a collapse of a system, a collapse of values, a collapse of sensibilities, indeed a collective blunting of sense of obligations..."[3] The feeble claim to efforts to overcome fear and its sources lies only in occasional self-destructive violent manifestations rather than a conscious and constructive long-term effort to demystify, overcome, and dominate fear. Devoid of any frame of decorous reference, individuals from this society tend to demonstrate their "courage" through reckless and absurd theatrical comportment when challenged by an unfamiliar environment. Imaginary historical heroism premised on violence serves as a collective mental therapy; and in this delusory state, the society does not stop to ask where the gains of this romanticised bravery have led it. Such a society has a long list of excuses why everything failed and continues to fail and why squirming in the face of fear continues to be the best strategy. It harbours and relishes its helplessness and victim-hood.

However, unlike its victim with (with its accepted "fate" of helplessness), fear is not static; it seeks to gain more grounds and to metamorphose from its overcome-able form into a real unassailable and formidable force. The victim-society inadvertently, through cowering, actively assists the metamorphosis of fear from its unreal state to a palpable, existing, and overwhelming monster.

A society that has chosen to live in fear fears everything and anything. It fears all odds, small and great, real and imaginary; it fears the consequences of even contemplating to tackle the odds, and it is even more frightened of the imaginary costs of challenging the odds. It draws up very vivid images of life-threatening scenarios if it attempts to change the energy dynamics between it and fear. The complicated elements of nature become objects of reverence. Invented taboos prohibit curiosity and the society lives at the mercy of natural and man-made phenomena. The society generates its own fear and limits its ability to overcome the occasional devastating effects of the elements. It seeks the easy way out, "the line of least resistance when faced with decisions that require the exertion of a moral will..."[4] It seeks to appease nature through sacrifices and rituals. Curiously, this fear and its associated taboos soon become identified as the traditional and cultural identity of this society. It becomes a way of life, dearly held on to, even when science has unequivocally unmasked the fear-inducing phenomena. This is an example of a self-induced *acquired* fear, unreal and inconsequential to the outsider, but a real and living menace to the victim-society.

The embattled society, depleted of useful collective energy by its profound fears, learns to appeal to and to draw on the goodwill of others to ensure its basic existence. It does not seek the goodwill to free itself from the clutches of fear; rather, it seeks outside support to alleviate the consequences of its self-induced helplessness in the face of fear. In exchange for this ready-made "support" and "solution", the desperate victim-society does not only gladly and prodigally part with its own available raw materials and other resources, but also does this at disparate and enslaving terms. Thus in exchange for reinforcing its cowering mechanisms at short term, this society creates other long-term fear-inducing factors. The provider of goodwill and the supposed Good Samaritan seizes on this feeble and desperate state of mind and imposes enslaving and very fearful terms on the beneficiaries of its largesse. A perpetual vicious cycle composing of fear as the main stakeholder, dependence as another major stakeholder and the victim-society as the stock is entrenched. In its occasional and shallow self-examination, the victim-society when not at a senseless internecine war, points fingers, not at itself, its ineptitude and intellectual lethargy but at others as it catches its fancy. It conveniently omits its role, its unfounded fears and its perpetually extended arms and puts all the blame on others who have learnt to master and conquer fear; and who have in turn, also constituted themselves into a source of fear for it. Rather than use whatever resources it gets under different self-abasing terms and pretexts to liberate itself from the clutches of fear, it further digs itself into the trenches and takes on new names like highly indebted poor country and indeed behaves like one. It resigns itself to martyrdom of circumstances and becomes a laboratory of social, political, and economic experiments. It becomes the guinea-pig of long conferences and seminars where everything except the gall-bladder that houses its fears is excised and substituted with alien transplants. It is no surprise that severe organ rejection begins as soon as the conference ends.

Fear fragments the society. The large society itself becomes a source of fear and members tend to group themselves into small units to ensure their survival. There are two main categories of regrouping of a phobic society. The first category is internally generated and is based on bloodline, clanhood and ethnicity. The second category is externally imposed (and avidly embraced) and has its origins in imposed boundaries, alien languages and religions. Rivalry between unrelated units is an important intra-unit cohesive factor. The rivalry is not a healthy competition in which any of the units seeks to overcome fear and pave the way for their development. It is rather directed at preserving the members of the group from the overall society fears. Each unit tends to perceive the other group as being responsible in part for their fears. In this fragmented state, the perception of the real source of fear becomes distorted, and the collective need to overcome it is undermined. Thus, the original society fear mutates and replicates itself in the fragments of the society. In its mutated state, fear becomes a tool of political, economic, and social management within this phobic society. The society's institutions search and find their roots in, and function on fear. Irrational violence, a sign of individual and collective helplessness and lack of resourcefulness manifests in all possible forms—subtle, overt, legal and illegal, and becomes a means of social communication and control.

There cannot be any kind of freedom in the presence of fear. Freedom abhors fear and vice versa. It is no gainsaying that political, economic, social freedoms and progress cannot exist in a fear-imbued society. In order to have other freedoms the society must first learn to liberate itself from the clutches of fear. It must seek the courage to conquer fear. This is the most important pillar of human and societal development. By dominating fear, the society shifts the energy balance in its favour and the pursuit of other freedoms becomes an attainable objective. When the reverse is attempted, that is, if the pursuit of other freedoms is *misunderstood* as liberating-from-fear strategy, not only is money wasted, a good deal of potentially useful energy and resources are also squandered. Chaos is the result of this misplacement of priority. It will then appear that the society in question is refractory to all forms of "assisted" development.

TREATING FEAR

Intractable under-development is a major consequence of resignation to "fate" in the face of odds. Fear depletes society's resourcefulness' capacity. Knowledge is limited to the mastery of others' outputs and the society is unable to generate adequate answers to its own problems. Some of the governments of the most under-developed (fear-incapacitated) societies in the world today are staffed by academics and scientists who have mastered other cultures' outputs. However, their knowledge and skills crumble under the weight of "fate" and self-induced helplessness of their societies.

The crippling toll of under-development, consequent upon its manifold phobias on a society demands that a solution be found to address the debilitating fears. If left untreated, phobias can have very dire consequences, as is the case with an individual. How then does one treat a society incapacitated by phobia? *What* kind of treatment can liberate it from fears of the known and the unknown, internally and externally generated factors of fear? In addition, *who* can liberate such a society from its fears and its consequences?

Can the treatment be found in throwing money at this society under any pretext? Can money help the society to overcome its fears? This is doubtful. If this external money helps bring about some transient changes in the society, the source of such money will, in time become an additional source of fear in itself. The society learns to add this source to its long list of fears. The strangling hold of the World Bank, the International Monetary Fund and the different money-lending clubs on their debtor nations is a good example. The immense burden and stress that African governments face in "justifying" funds allocated by United Nations' multiple agencies and their diverse funding systems have become a source of concern even for this organisation. A fear-debilitated society caught in this complicated web of dependency dreads the consequences of losing these funds, and it further digs itself into the trenches, giving more grounds to fear. Moreover, the managers of this money (the government) may in turn use this money to create more internal fear-inducing factors. A new chain of fear is thus established. The local managers of money fear the distant source; the rest of the society fears the managers of the money.

Can the treatment of society phobia be found in an imported socio-philosophical prescription? This is also doubtful. The exporters of such solutions like to use their society as a reference of successful treatment of fear. They seek, and readily find analogies between the fears that their society underwent at a particular time in its history and what the other society is undergoing. These similarities (the symptoms) end in their being identical as symptoms. The time and space of the events (the underlying cause of the illness) culminating in the emergence of these fears in the two societies under comparison are completely different. However, the doctor-society conveniently overlooks this fact in its self-deluding bid to *cure* the sick society. Thus, the imported prescriptions are directed at the symptoms in the hope that by curing the symptoms, the underlying cause of illness will *somehow* disappear. Experience has however shown that, when and if one symptom disappears, two or more new ones take its place. The doctor-society becomes baffled and again searches for another symptom-directed treatment, with or without the consent of the patient-society. After many trials of different treatments, the doctor-society, confounded by its failures, threatens the sick society to either get well on any of its treatments or face the consequences of doctor-fatigue. The sick society, high and confused on multiple concoctions of treatments soon adds the dread of doctor-fatigue to its list of fears. Fear gains more grounds.

Sometimes, a more sympathetic doctor-society or doctor-entity engages the services of some members of the sick society to diagnose the underlying cause and to search for a cure for the society. These members of the society, consequent upon their individual and collective fears quickly learn to see their society through the mirrors of the doctor-entity. They parrot the views of their employers (views, which the employers actually want to do away with) and thus fail to help the employers have an insight into the underlying problems. They reinforce the perception of the helplessness of the situation and convince the doctor-entity of the correctness of its approach. Armed with autochthon approval of the appropriateness of its approach, the doctor-entity congratulates itself on its diagnosis and approach, and puts enormous resources at the disposal of the sick society. They soon learn that they have only been treating the most insignificant symptom of a more profound problem.

Can the treatment be found in an imported political ideology? The appropriateness of an imported political ideology to address the problems of a fear-imbued society is debatable. Any political ideology takes its roots from the historical and philosophical specificity of its country or society of origin. It evolves to address the philosophy of life and the way of life of the society in question. It is tailor-made for that society. It is not an export material under any guise. The importation of a foreign-born ideology by a fear-afflicted society to address its phobias, and the consequences of this defeatist strategy are glaring symptoms of the magnitude of the power-balance in favour of fear in that society. It is a sign of intellectual laziness, a proof that the society has very little energy for resourcefulness. It seeks a ready-made solution, an easy way out. Not unexpectedly, this imported solution fails to cure the sick society of its fears. Confounded by their failure, and obsessed with keeping themselves in power, the managers of the society (importers of ideas) convert this ideology into an instrument of fear. The exporters of the ideology, who seek to re-create others in their own image or to execute their not-so hidden agenda, go to great lengths to keep the importers of ideology in power. The reckless support of murderous regimes in Africa by belligerent ideologues of the cold war is a case in point. As is the case with the use of money as treatment, this ideological export-import strategy creates a new chain of fear in the phobic society.

Can the solution be found in religion? Members of a phobic society tend to look for individual solutions in religions. They flock to places of worship in search for individual way-out of the collective fear. This is another proof of the lack of energy reserves for resourcefulness. Through religion, they seek miracles to make fears disappear. They invest the little existential energy left to them in worship and leave things to take their course according to the dictates of "heaven". The managers of religions aggravate the fear of their flocks by adding heavenly fears to their already long list of earthly fears. People adhere to religion because of fears and religion reinforces their fears and even adds to it. Fear again gains grounds on the religious front.

Civil societies, realising the debilitating effect of fear on development, advocate individual and collective empowerment. The word "empowerment" is however not clearly defined by its *professional* users and is loosely employed as a catchword, a fanciful rhetoric with diverse, colourful, and sometimes far from reality concept. Taken to its fullness, empowerment means overcoming fear, and when pursued as such, it provides the only plausible way out of the vicious fear-society energy imbalance. Unfortunately, however, this philosophy is confronted with many obstacles deliberately or inadvertently engineered by the advocates of empowerment on one hand and the victims of fear on the other hand. In being cautious not to offend the local sensibilities, the advocates of empowerment tend to leave out the most profound fear-inducing factors and deal only on the surface. Serious empowerment advocates that have at one time or the other attempted to go beyond the permissible surface have been accused of wanting to demystify the local culture, impose their own philosophy of life, and thus hold their beneficiaries to ransom. In other words, local interests tend to see and portray these advocates as having a hidden neo-colonising and acculturating agenda. The victim-society's historical experience of oppression and injustices under different pretexts (trade, religion, civilizing missions, etc.) constitutes a major obstacle to this empowerment philosophy. Although, the history of fear-gripped society moves in circles and keeps repeating itself, the people, unaware of this fact are unwilling to consciously contribute to a re-enactment of their difficult past experiences. They are unconvinced even with the most powerful of arguments and are distrustful of any foreign abstract (to them) concept that does not address their immediate needs. This plays into the hands of the government which is innately reticent to see its people liberated from some of the fears, which it has also put in place. It fears a change in power-balance between it and the people it governs. The government dreads a situation whereby it becomes the only victim of fear of its foreign friends on one hand, and of its people on the other hand.

The "what" as regards empowerment as a liberating philosophy is clear, however, the appropriate "how" constitutes a major challenge. Many see the "how" in human rights' promotion and enforcement; however, many obstacles confront this point of view. There is no doubt that universal respect of the concept of human rights without double standards may reassure members of phobic societies and lay bare the irrelevance of their fears. However, the skewed demand of obligations by the impunible advocates of human rights who flout the same rights at will when their interests are *perceived* to be threatened constitutes another source of fear for phobia-gripped societies. Such societies in their fragile state want to know what moral rights do these impunible flouters of human rights have to impose their lopsided dictates and demands on others. Rather than seeing it as a liberating philosophy that can be modified, if only to have the freedom to overcome fear and thus acquire other freedoms, the phobic society sees another mangling manacle being waved about by the proponents of human rights. How can a Black African, who is ridiculed, humiliated, and attacked by skinheads in the streets of St. Petersburg with the tacit consent of the authorities, believe in universal human rights? Which member of his family and his community will believe in the altruism of the proponents of human rights who come to preach "rights" in his village of origin? How can anyone expect that people of fear-gripped societies will be liberated from their fears through flagrant, skewed, and double standard human rights philosophy? While the principle in its letters may inspire hope on paper, the lopsided, double-standard practice of it by the powers that be, and the reckless violations under different pretexts by these same "implacable" advocates, portend distrust and engender dread of a new enslavement strategy. The non-adherence of some countries to the International Court of Justice system and the convenient lopsided interpretation of human rights in favour of the powerful and mighty cannot inspire confidence in fear-afflicted societies. From the point of view of these societies, human rights become an issue when for any reason they or their leaders are *judged* as "infractors" and impunity casually becomes the rule under the pretext of "national security" (which is an exclusive right of some), when the same rights are infringed upon by the mighty and powerful. These fear-afflicted societies, already toiling and desperate under their long list of fears can only see another devious trap of fear. An absurd logic of "if the mighty and powerful have the right to pervert justice, we have the right to remain captives of fear, but we will not add their human rights to our list of fears" thus becomes a way of life. The resistance (under different pretexts) of the Organization of African Unity and its constituent countries to recognise the Universal Declaration of Human Rights for many years is a case in point.

Perhaps the most successful empowerment campaign in Black Africa until date has been senghorian negritude philosophy. Though fraught with inconsistencies and undesirable declarations that put it at loggerheads with many African scholars, it had a mind-liberating impact on the general populace who could not be bothered with complicated intellectual arguments between scholars. It put pride in the mind of many Africans and taught them that there was no challenge too tough for the black race. It successfully gave back dignity to the discountenanced black race. No other African scholar has had such a subtle but strong, non-confrontational mind-liberating impact on Black Africans. Rather being re-worked and further developed, this mind-liberating philosophy has been quietly laid to rest. Some literatures claim that it has lost its relevance! This is another typical characteristic of societies suffering from fear. They do not recognise their heroes and their works; and when the heroes are resilient, these societies go to great lengths to ridicule and destroy them along with their legacies. Mind-liberating leaders like Kwame Nkrumah, Patrice Lumumba, and Thomas Sankara who sought to lead the people in the battle to overcome fear were violently removed and their legacy quietly laid to rest. The mindless burning of Kwame Nkrumah's papers after the coup in 1966 was an indication of the fact that fear also holds any form of constructive reasoning captive.

The continued relevance of civil societies in Africa in years to come depends among many other things, on their ability and resourcefulness to translate their *empowerment* philosophy into a real shift of energy balance between this fear-afflicted continent and fear, in favour of the continent. In other words, their *beneficiaries* acquire the courage to demystify any form of fear and find their own appropriate solutions.

Fear induces stress on the society; the longer the society harbours fear, the more chronic the stress and its consequences on the development and the way of life of the society. In the face of trans-generational stress, a society either reorganises itself to overcome the stress by harnessing little reserves of collective energy towards resourcefulness and creativity in order to ensure its survival and add quality to its existence, or it redefines its way of life to accommodate and live with the stress. When a society chooses the former option, an appropriate management of knowledge acquired from the first attempt to harness the energy reserves has a direct multiplying effect on the amount of energy available for development. The more the energy acquired by this society from the society-fear energy system, the less the amount of energy in favour of fear and the less the stress on the society. This type of society begins to *emerge* towards what is universally known as *development*.

The society may however feel overwhelmed by fear and may resign itself to self-imposed helplessness. In such a situation, the creative energy is expended on unproductive endeavours, and the society learns to depend on the meagre goodwill of others. The society takes the minimum necessary energy needed for survival from the society-fear energy system and resigns itself to the chronic fear-induced stress. However, as already argued, the fear component in the society-fear energy system is not static; it evolves rapidly with changes in internal and external environments and seeks to pull more energy towards itself. A society that finds itself in this situation is compelled to struggle for the energy necessary for its basic survival. It has to evolve minimal coping mechanisms or it will face extinction. These minimal coping mechanisms constitute a form of accommodative adaptation to stress. They are not directed at overcoming stress and cannot be used as stress-eliminating tools; rather they are directed at ensuring the basic survival of the society in question. This accommodative adaptation is however at a cost to the society. In order to ensure its survival, the society has to redefine itself. The being has to be redefined. Life, a continuum of periods of life—childhood, young adulthood, adulthood, middle age, and old age is redefined with corresponding redefinition of the constituent periods. Many refer to this kind of society as "developing" or underdeveloped. It is however not clear what "developing" means in this case. It is rather a "disappearing" society. Sub-Sahara Africa belongs to this group of fear-afflicted societies that, in the face of fear, has chosen accommodative adaptation as a survival strategy. Fear occupies a large part of the African existence and experience, and Africa has not been able to demonstrate any capacity to deal with it.

FEAR IN SUB-SAHARA AFRICA

A black African newborn is probably one of the most courageous human beings in the world. He has overcome all the possible odds in his nine months of uterine life to see the light of the day. Even the process of his birth is a major feat that if transposed on any adult-life challenge, will require the most courageous adult to surmount the odds and live to tell the story. The newborn is born with in-built survival mechanisms. Having overcome all the odds of intra-uterine life and the perilous process of his birth, he comes into the world, endowed with an innate ability to overcome fears and to surmount the comparatively less challenging odds of life. However, his instinct to survive and live well soon becomes captive of the acquired fears of his environment. The family and the society teach him that the fear of fear is the beginning of wisdom. He is immediately constrained by family and community taboos, founded on their fear of the known and the unknown. He inherits, and is soon held captive by internally generated fears which include cultural fears, fear of the environment and the elements, religious fears, institutional fears, distrust and fear of others, and to this list, he learns to add his own individual fears. Paradoxically, the only thing that he is taught not to fear is time; the only thing that really puts his exist-ence at peril. He soon learns that a village hill is "sacred" and cannot be climbed because of "evil spirits" on top of the hill; or that a river passing at the edge of the village must be worshipped and sacrifices must be made to appease it in order to continue to flow or not to flood the village. The list of fear induced-taboos is endless, and a fearless child soon becomes a captive of fear like his forerunners. These fear-induced taboos define the philosophy of life of the com-munity. Courage is redefined within the limits of commu-nity-imposed taboos and is premised only on ensuring basic survival. The community (deliberately or unconsciously) does not recognise, or chooses to ignore the rights of the individual to chal-lenge these taboos, a feat that may improve the quality of his life and by proxy bring positive changes to the community. The community sets the limits of challenge and courage, and its members are obliged to conform.

Sometimes, these fears are not unfounded. In some instances, they are predicated on lived experience, and in other cases, a small group of people introduced these fears as community-control tools in order to protect the interests of the group. However, whatever may be the origin of these fears, they become sacrosanct with time, and constitute a way of life of the community in the name of culture and tradition. Any member of the community that challenges the "sacredness" of these fears either is considered "mad" or becomes an untouchable outcast. In certain cases, sentences of mysterious pun-ishments and maledictions, including death (often helped by human hands) hang over anyone who attempts to demystify or chal-lenge these fear-induced taboos. Ironically, these fear-induced taboos only apply to members of the society of origin; it does not apply to foreigners who for one reason or the other have come to temporarily reside in this society. It is not an uncommon sight in Africa that so-called strict all-male cults from which the local women are excluded at the pain of death are rolled out as "cultural activities" to visiting women from other cultures. Moreover, there is no cult too important or so sacred that the African will not roll out to foreign journalists and visitors irrespective of their sex. These internally generated fears and their taboo appendages only serve to repress creative challenges that can improve the quality of life of the local people. Rather than evolve to match the exigencies of the fast-changing world, these fears are caste in iron. The power-cabal among the Africans, afraid of losing their hold on the people, keeps the centuries-old flame of fear alive among the people. It is interesting to note that western education has no influence whatsoever on this kind of self-induced phobia. Many Black Africans living outside the shores of Africa make annual trips back to their villages of origin to "celebrate" these fears. And many that live in other parts (away from "home", even if less than a hundred kilometres) of the geographical entity called their "country" also make the annual trip back home to reaffirm their commitments to stay within the limits of age-old fears. This is not an attempt to discredit or demystify peoples' cultures and traditions. All human beings have the right to develop and keep their culture, but when any culture or tradition fails to evolve and visibly handicaps the development of the people, then, it should come under question. Fear and its taboo mate kill creative mind-liberating curiosity and inhibit the natural human instinct to invent ways to overcome adversity. A fear-afflicted society lives with "what" and its consequences; fear (and the continuous reengineering of it by certain interest groups) does not permit, and in many cases forbids the members of the society to ask "why" and "how".

Internally generated fears, as already argued become venerated taboos. An example of this kind of fear-induced taboo is found in a still-existing chiefdom in a mountainous African country. The chiefs whose homes or palaces are situated on top of the mountains are forbidden by tradition to descend the mountain. They cannot visit their subjects that live in the valleys and on the plains. According to "tradition", any chief that flouts this tradition will die. Everyone believed and still believes without asking questions. Why would a king, a mortal like any of his subjects die if he came down from his mountain home? What will kill him? A supernatural cause or a man-assisted "supernatural" cause? The "what" and its consequence became the tradition and no one ever bothered to ask "why" or "how". The system of governance (and any development it could have brought about) was hampered by this taboo for centuries. It was eventually found out that the people living on top of the mountains, including the chief himself had no exposure-induced natural immunity to malaria because there were no mosquitoes, hence malaria at the altitude where they lived. Thus, if they came down to the plains, which had many mosquitoes and caught malaria, the course of the disease was more fulminant than in the inhabitants of the plains and invariably ended in death of the victim. *Someone else* deciphered the "why". In spite of this knowledge, and the availability of malarial prophylaxis, people still hold on dearly to this "tradition".

The other group of fears, into which the African child is born, has its roots in the collective experience of Africans in their relationship with the outside world. This group of fears self-multiplies and self-sustains. Both the local power-cabal and their people are at the mercy of these fears. This group of externally generated fears includes the elements, diseases (like malaria), pernicious exploitation (including slavery, colonialism, and neo-colonialism) by people from other cultures and imported religions. These fears are characterised by their uncanny ability to self-propagate exponentially in a society already weakened by its internally generated fears. As is the case with fear-induced taboos, the "what" and the consequences of these fears are the only considered factors. The people, heavily burdened by their own internally generated fears do not even have the energy to question the "why" and "how" of the externally induced fears. It is impossible to produce a response to overcome any source of fear if the "how" and "why" are not put under scrutiny. The African society has suffered and continues to suffer from this error. Sub-Sahara Africa has paid and continues to pay dearly with the lives of its citizens, its resources, and will possibly pay with its future for this oversight.

The obsession with "what" and a complete disregard of "why" and "how" in the face of adversity can be illustrated with events that occurred during the three-hundred years of transatlantic slavery to which sub-Sahara Africa was subjected. We will look at one of the methods by which people were caught and sold off, and we will analyse the reaction of the African society to this method. One favourite method of slave catchers was to set fire to the thatched houses in the village under siege. People rushed out of their houses and were rounded up by the slave catchers, bound in chains, and matched to the coast to be sold to their European clients. In some instances, the slave catchers painted themselves in chalk to acquire grotesque appearance, which served to immobilise (with fear!) those who had rushed out of their burning huts and to facilitate rounding them up. This method, among others was used for nearly three hundred years. In a society not imbued with fear, one would expect that the people would take measures to construct not-easily-flammable houses; that they would direct their mental and natural resources at inventing counter-measures. If this had happened, maybe less people would have lost their lives and maybe less people would have been taken away in slavery, or maybe the period would have been much shorter. This however did not happen. The same thatched houses or mud houses with thatched roofs that facilitated the work of the slavers still litter the African landscape until today. Some may want to argue that the African way of building is premised on the

climate and that the African is an outdoors person. They may further argue that this form of building is environment-friendly. This
argument is not only devoid of any logic in the face of the damage
that this form of habitation caused in terms of slavery, but it is also a
futile exercise to justify the unjustifiable. It reeks of a condescending
attempt to condone complacency in the face of adversity and does
not in anyway do justice to the effort to challenge Africa to rise up
to redeem itself. The apologists of this line of thought will concur
that today, one can find *some* brick and mortar houses in many rural
villages. The question that a true African should ask is why did it
take so long for these houses to begin to appear on the African landscape? Moreover, why were Africans, who faced serious adversity
because of the nature of their houses, not the avant-gardes of house
construction revolution with the immense natural resources at their
disposal? Some Africanists will argue that Mali was at the forefront
of building revolution in Africa, and that the multi-storey mud
houses in Timbuktu attest to this. This argument merits to be analysed in the face of the fact that on transposing this period of Mali
Empire on contemporary Africa, one discovers a stunning parallel.
It is a historical fact that *some* houses in Mali Empire were made of
mud and straw. Timbuktu was famous for this; it was the capital.
Outside Timbuktu, people lived in thatched houses, at the mercy of
the elements and slavers. The same is the case in most of contemporary African societies today. Contemporary African governments go
the extra mile to build "befitting capitals". Multi-million dollar
high-rise buildings, expensive villas, beautiful tarred roads,
many-star hotels, cafès, highbrow restaurants, and many self-deluding white elephant structures fashioned after their metropole make
up the city centre. On travelling a few miles out of the city, one
finds that a large part of the population still lives in the same conditions as their ancestors did many centuries ago. Thus, it is logical to
pose the question that when one talks of Africa, (either as an Afri-

canist or an external observer committed to Africa), to which Africa and to what Africans should we make reference? There is no doubt that we should source our reference in the teeming population of the fear-imbued oppressed people and not in the myopic political bourgeoisie either in Timbuktu or in any contemporary African capital. Herein lies the source of conflict between a western-educated African and the external observer; the educated African seeks and finds his reference in the landmarks of the circumscribed surreal environment of the African bourgeoisie, while the external observer looks at the same society at large, sees the condemned, peripheral teeming mass of people and draws his mental image of Africa. Irrespective of whatever arguments or excuses employed by different interest groups, the fact remains that there are no documented concerted efforts to review the nature of houses people lived in, in order to thwart the arson tactics of slavers.

Following three hundred years of slavery-induced fears and consequences, the continent was subjected to colonialism for another hundred years. Colonialism did not only aggressively introduce a new set of fears into the society; it also actively sought to perpetuate this fear through a gradual mental re-engineering of the colonised peoples. It created the fear of unity in sub-Sahara Africa in order to facilitate neo-colonialism, the next phase, or next package of fears for Africans. Kwame Nkrumah, at the founding conference of the Organisation of African Unity in May 1963 warned the African leaders of the dangers of creating favourable environment for a new generation of fears. He called on Africans to "unite or to perish". He, passionately, and with vision called on his colleagues to overcome the fear of unity. No one listened; if they heard him at all, their individual fears and externally-induced fears had gained so much ground in their minds that they could not see the "why" and "how" and the consequences of fear which Kwame Nkrumah graphically painted to them. In the Accra summit of 1965, Nkrumah again repeated his call and as he did in 1963, gave a blueprint on the advantages of overcoming the fear of unity. No one heeded him.

An important fear that evolved in the course of the contact of the African with the foreigner and his consequent mental reengineering is the fear of truth. We live in the age of fear of truth, where a *truth-activist* is a pariah, an undesirable element. A good example of the fear of truth was the reaction or inaction of the founding fathers of Africa to Kwame Nkrumah's warning on the dangers of *balkanised* (along colonial lines) Africa. The late Julius Nyerere on the occasion of the fortieth anniversary of the "independence" of Ghana in March 1997, confirmed that it was *fear* (nurtured by a large majority of leaders present in Addis Abeba in 1963) that neutralised Nkrumah's vision. In his speech, he said "..Kwame Nkrumah underestimated the degree of suspicion and animosity which his crusading passion had created among a substantial number of his fellow heads of state.., the *fear* of a number of us to lose our precious status was quite palpable[5]".

It is no over-statement that sub-Sahara Africa is now in the clutches of neo-colonialism-induced fears, as was foreseen by Kwame Nkrumah. In his speech in 1963 in Addis, he said, "We must unite…or perish". This is an impending prophesy—Africa failed to unite in 1963 and 1965, and the imminence of the consequence of this historical failure was not lost on Kwame Nkrumah who shared it with his fellow presidents.

Africa has undergone three phases of externally induced fears (slavery, colonialism, and neo-colonialism) and failed to learn anything from the experience. If we apply the theory of Human Energy Pole (HEP) to the future of Africa, then it is evident that the next phase is probably the *extinction* of sub-Sahara Africa (Kwame Nkrumah's prophesy of perishing). This does not necessarily mean the extinction of the black race. The disappearance of sub-Sahara African peoples will come in form of their dispersion, their displacement (from Africa) and their scattering as small politically unimportant minorities among other cultures even here on African soil. And the process has already innocuously begun! The future depopulation of Sub-Sahara Africa in some years to come has become, albeit unwittingly, a favourite "discovery" by "experts" from all the corners of the world except from Africa. In different ways, and using different forms, they announce the imminent demise of Sub-Sahara Africans. For example, climatologists claim that Africa will be at the severe receiving end of global warming, not only because of the effect of this phenomenon on agricultural outputs, but also because of exponential increase in number of cases of infectious diseases like Malaria, HIV/AIDS, and Tuberculosis. Experts in infectious diseases yearly publish astronomical figures of Black Africans who have died the previous year, or who will die in the coming year from a wide range of diseases. When all these "expert" predictions and declarations are put together and added on to the senseless wars and killings that happen on the African soil, it becomes apparent that a severe depopulation of Africa is already underway, and we are simply not aware of it.

It is paradoxical that under the heavy and highly-mediatised apocalyptic disease burden and violent deaths in Africa, another group of "experts" claims that the population figures of Africa are on the increase! "Experts" many a time are too highly absorbed with their "areas of specialisation" and with themselves to know what "experts" in other fields, even located next door to them are saying. They treat their "facts" as if they were unrelated and as if they were referring to different groups of peoples. No one bothers to put these facts together to deduce the *real aggregate* effects of these "facts" on Sub-Sahara Africans. This deliberate or negligent gap in information management and knowledge chain plays into the hands of the political elite, who prefers to choose and use (more favourable for their purposes) data. The import of their criminal negligence of the present on the future generations of Africans is lost on the political elite. Rather than tackle this problem with vision, self-serving African political elite's vision is limited to self-enrichment and perpetuating themselves in power. Besides the glamour of having the power and wielding it to cower dissenting voices, the African political elite has not shown any signs of a carefully thought-out and focused commitment to reverse the dire fortunes of the black race. Padded census figures are not only useful tools for corruption, but also serve to demand aid and debts from their "international community friends".

Kwame Nkrumah said it and it is beginning to happen without Africans giving a thought to it. Contrary to the misconceived expectation of a cataclysmic event, the process of depopulation and subsequent reduction to politically unimportant minorities that failed to happen during three hundred years of slavery and more than a hundred years of colonisation has begun insidiously. The process is gaining steam under the malicious marginalisation of Africans from the human mainstream (except as a reminding sample of what not to aspire to be).

Ironically, while the African is a willing and compliant depository of all imaginable fears that threaten his existence, the only thing that he does not fear (and which puts his survival in great danger) is time. Many scholars and non-scholars have studied and written numerous papers and books on the African concept of time. In ignorance, Africans themselves proudly refer to their self-destructive positioning within the universal space and time that define the existence of our universe as "African time". It is absurd that the African deliberately disregards the only thing that will cost him dearly in the fast-changing world. Rather than admonish the African peoples of this counter-productive and self-destructive mental attitude, African intellectuals write "academic papers" on the African concept of time and go to great lengths to justify the African perception of his position in space and time. This is defending the un-defendable. Africans, to whom time has been cruel in their history, and are, therefore lagging behind the rest of the world, cannot afford to play with time. Neither can they afford to continue to romanticise time concepts that have become completely obsolete in the fast changing world. If Africa wants to catch up with the rest of the world, then, it has to change its attitude to time. As a matter of survival, Africans at this period of their history need to place more value on time than any other culture in the world.

DEVELOPMENT = 1/ EXPLOITATION X FEAR^2
$(D = 1/EF^2)^6$

Development or the lack of it is defined by certain universally accepted parameters. Societies are categorised as developed or underdeveloped when measured against these standards, which are defined by certain indicators. In order to be acceptable to all, these indicators must measure *factual effects* of development or underdevelopment. Ironically, however, these indicators, when applied to underdeveloped societies, largely tend to measure *deductive effects*, based on certain predetermined conditions. These predetermined conditions include "poor governance", "corruption", and infamous geographical location. From the point of view of pundits, any society with any combination of the three conditions *cannot* be considered as developed. In other words, the *effects* are *deduced* from predetermined *conditioning causes* (real and imaginary).

For example, it is claimed that the absence of good governance and corruption are major root causes of underdevelopment, and high infant mortality rate is an important indicator of underdevelopment. We can analyse this position using infant mortality rate as an example:

Condition I:	Poor Governance.
Condition II:	Pervasive corruption.
Condition III:	Infamous geographical location.
Cause:	Non-functional health system.
Deductive effect:	High infant mortality rate.

In other words, a country that for some reason does not practice "acceptable" form of governance is bound to have high infant mortality rate. This skewed neo-narcissistic logic of self-acclaimed democrats (left, right and centre) ascribes pre-determined *symptoms* to societies, which do not fit into their model of socio-political order. This maxim implicitly implies that the "development" claimed by developed countries is hinged on a good system of "governance" with little or no corruption. The logic is dismally fallible because it fails to take cognisance of recent history as illustrated by the case of the former Soviet Union. For example, under today's definition of "good governance", the former Soviet Union would not have been recognised as a country with good system of governance; however, the infant mortality rate in the ex-socialist republic during its existence was comparable to that of western countries with "good governance". Thus, the root-causes of underdevelopment do not lie in poor system of governance. Poor system of governance is a symptom of a more profound problem.

The role of fear in underdevelopment has been discussed in previous chapters. The combination of exploitation (internal or external) and fear are major setbacks for development of any society and they constitute the root causes of underdevelopment. Exploitation in this case is defined broadly as **any direct or indirect conscious** action or design, subtle or crude, pacific or violent, orchestrated to usurp, to dispossess, to steal, to manipulate or to beg for, under false pretences from a group of people all forms of resources (including the mind of the exploited) to which the exploiter has no moral rights to under natural laws. There is an inverse relationship between development on one hand, and fear and exploitation on the other hand as the hypothetical equation below shows:

$$\textbf{Development} = \textbf{1/Exploitation X Fear}^2$$

The more the fear or exploitation, the less the chances of development of a society. Moreover, there is a direct relationship between fear and exploitation. All forms of fear abound in situations of exploitation. Fear serves as an instrument to facilitate exploitation; and exploitation flourishes in an atmosphere of fear. Fear provides a field of play for manipulation, and exploitation and manipulation reinforce fear. If however, there were no exploitation and the only denominator is fear, one can deduce from the equation above that such a society would be much better off than another where exploitation increases the denominator and reduces the level of development.

The hypothesis inherent in this equation is based on the certain assumptions:

1. Varied levels of internal exploitation exist in all societies. These levels are graded on a rising scale of 1-10. The higher the exploitation, the higher the number on the scale.

2. Varied levels of fear exist in all societies. These levels are graded on a rising scale of 1-10. The higher the fear, the higher the number on the scale.

3. Therefore, the denominator in the equation can never have a value of zero.

4. Consequently, development cannot be infinite.

We shall consider two different societies (Society A and Society B) for the purposes of illustration of this hypothesis. In the case of Society A, the society makes huge investments in fear-overcoming skills and technology (and thus, largely dominates fear) and puts enormous human and material resources to reduce exploitation by others (outsiders) to the minimum. For this society, we shall attribute 2 points to exploitation and 1 point to fear. The equation thus reads:

Development: $1/2X1^2 = 0.5$

In society B however, there are no fear-overcoming skills and technology; the society depends on foreign aid, several multinationals are exploiting the natural resources, and the society is caught in a web of debts. We shall attribute 7 points to exploitation and 8 points to fear. The result will be:

Development: $1/7X8^2 = 0.002$

From the example above, one can see that society A is 224 times more developed than society B. It is however important to note that very often, a "developed" society like society A, has not only used the resources of society B in the quest to overcome its fears, but has also deliberately kept society B exploitable through many devices like debts, political interference, deprivation of capital, commodity-price manipulation, and trade imbalance.

How then, can we calculate fear and exploitation indices? In order to determine the Fear Index, the following constitute some indicators that can be developed, and for which mathematical values can be ascribed (as is done with Corruption index):

1. External aid per GDP

2. External interference in political orientation

3. Debts

4. External interference in national economic and social policy formulation,

5. Trade imbalances

6. Number of multinationals in the country

7. Employment policy of multinationals,

8. Tax payment by multinationals,

9. Income declaration by multinationals.

In the same manner, Exploitation Index can be calculated from several indicators derived from the above definition of exploitation.

Sub-Sahara Africa is a victim of not only its fears, but also of external manipulation and exploitation. There is no doubt that Africa has been a victim of all forms of exploitation for more than a thousand years. The continent has been greedily plundered for its human and natural resources, and the fact that Africa still possesses immense wealth is an indication that the continent is probably the richest in the world. Other cultures that were subjected to similar pernicious exploitation are now faced with extinction.

Those that came to Africa to exploit it came armed with intents and with instruments of fear to facilitate their exploitation. Looking back into history, the Arabs, from the eighth century brought their religion in exchange for slaves, gold, salt, and dyes. They exchanged one horse for fifteen to twenty Africans. Religion in this case was the instrument of fear. When the Africans refused to change their ways, the Arabs came armed, on horse-backs, to *convert* and in the process, they freely helped themselves to the resources of the victims of their swords and indeed to many survivors that neither they nor anyone can account for their whereabouts till present day. Africans quickly learnt to add the "pious" Arabs, their religion and their religious forays to the list of their fears. The Sultan of Oman, astounded by the vastness of the booty and pleased with the ease with which his instruments of fear overpowered and browbeat Africans into parting with their resources (human and material) transferred the capital of his kingdom to Zanzibar in order to personally, and at close quarters, oversee the plunder. When we apply the Development Equation to this documented historical situation, we will see that Arabs multiplied the fears of Africans and used the opportunity to exploit them. If Africans were at a certain level of development before the arrival of Arabs, the exploitation by Arabs and the instrument of fear, which they brought along with them, damaged the pre-existing development and set the Africans back considerably.

Another major landmark in African history is Transatlantic Slavery that lasted over three hundred years. This catastrophe sent Africa deep into the dark recesses of underdevelopment, from which it is yet to recover. Let us imagine that the development index (as calculated from the equation above) of Africa before transatlantic slavery was **0.1**. Slavery was exploitation at its cruellest from, so we will give it 9 on the Exploitation Index Scale. If we imagined for a moment the fear experienced by Africans from the burning down of their villages, to the march to the coast, the wanton killing of some "undesirables" and to the trip across the ocean, then, attributing 10 to fear on the Fear Index Scale would be a just exercise. Thus during and after three hundred years of slavery, the Development Index of Africa plunged down to:

$$\textbf{Development: } 1/9 \text{X} 10^2 = 1/900 = 0.001$$

The colonisation of African territory that followed in the wake of slavery kept African human and society development at this level and prepared it for the "post-independence" re-colonisation by neo-liberal economic policies and political agenda. It is paradoxical that the same people who were, and are still responsible for the underdevelopment of Africa now accuse the continent of contributing less than 1% to world economy, and they write great volumes on all possible imaginary reasons why Africa is underdeveloped, conveniently forgetting their malevolent incursion and ruthless plunder of the continent.

This however, is not an attempt to make a case for Africa to resign itself to this fate and point fingers. Africans should point fingers at themselves and self-analyse what their role has been in bringing Africa to this lamentable state. Africans leaders and elites, from the first contact with Arabs through this period of neo-colonialism have, through their tacit consent or active participation exposed their subjects to exploitation, humiliation, and hardship in the hands of people from other cultures. In the face of adversity, they denied and continue to deny the people the necessary leadership to overcome fears and in many cases, they even constitute themselves into sources of fear.

LIVING WITH
ADVERSITY

A phobic society with abysmal Development Index (as discussed in the previous chapter) that adopts a self-induced helplessness in the face of adversities may manifest its reaction in two ways. It may choose to ignore the adversities, believing that they will somehow disappear, or it may choose to redefine its way of life and *the self (its being)* to the harsh realities that surround it. Whatever the choice is, this society faces a possible extinction unless it changes its "helplessness" attitude. In the former case, the extinction is rapid, while in the latter, it may be spread over many years.

Sub-Sahara Africa appears to have made the choice of redefinition of its way of life and its existence in order to survive. We shall use the world statistics of Life Expectancy to prove this position. The Unicef in its 2005 State of World Children Report made a comparison of increase in life expectancy in different regions of the world over a thirty-three year period (1970 and 2003). Sub-Sahara Africa made a net-gain of only 2 years in life expectancy (from 44 years in 1970 to 46 years in 2003) within this period. Latin America and the Caribbean regions made a net-gain of 10 years (from 60 years in 1970 to 70 years in 2003), and the world average moved from 56 years in 1970 to 63 years in 2003. The Chart below compares the net-gains made in life expectancy by different regions of the world during this period:

Chart 1[7]:

Life Expectancy in different parts of the world

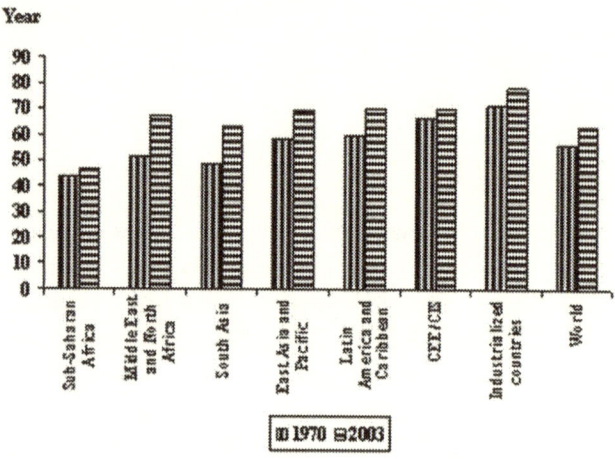

The chart above shows that Sub-Sahara Africa is critically lagging behind the rest of the world in life expectancy. In other words, Sub-Sahara Africa is paying for its notorious *helplessness* in the face of fears and exploitation with a reduced life span. Fear also made it impossible for the continent to make any improvements to this lamentable state. If Sub—Sahara Africa was only able to improve its life expectancy by only two years before the era of neo-liberal political ideology with its strangulating free market economic policies, then, it is not difficult to imagine that the life expectancy curve will probably take a nose-dive in years to come when this frightening double-standard ideology is imposed fully as the ruling world order.

People and cultures have disappeared before in human history and the disappearance of Sub-Sahara Africa (not physically from the map) will be just a matter of time. Self-serving pundits with questionable agenda have a ready list of woes and calamities (except fear and exploitation) to explain why Africa is in this situation. They choose to ignore that these woes and calamities are symptoms of more profound problems.

Faced with a reduced lifespan, the African redefines the different periods of lifecycle to accommodate his biological and social needs. Universally, childhood is defined as the first eighteen years of life. When this universal definition is applied to Sub-Sahara Africa, it means that the African is left with 28 years (out of his life expectancy of 46 years) to go through the period of young-adulthood, adulthood, middle age and the period of old age. The chart below shows the life-cycle deficit that the African is confronted with in this situation:

Chart 2[8]:

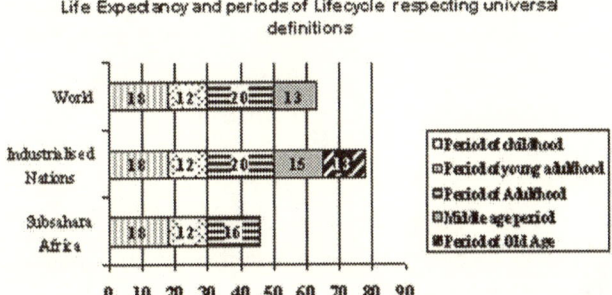

If life in Sub-Sahara Africa were to be lived according to the standards shown in the chart above, the lifecycle deficit will imply an accelerated extinction of this society. Consciously or unconsciously, the Sub-Saharan African society redefined the different periods of life (under different pretexts—religious, traditional, economic, cultural, illiteracy, etc.) to compensate for this deficit. The chart below compares the re-definition of different periods of lifecycle by Sub-Sahara Africa with those of industrialised countries:

Chart 3[9]:

Redefinition of different periods of Lifecycle in Sub-Sahara Africa.

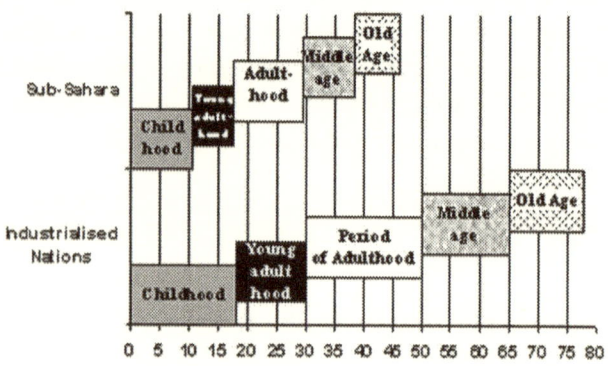

The above chart shows the shortened periods of lifecycle that Sub-Sahara Africa has adopted to compensate for its short lifespan. From this chart, one observes that the period of childhood is reduced from the universally accepted age of 18 years to 11 years. Okot p'Bitek in his Song of Lawino describes this life-cycle readjustment in the following words:

"A person's age is seen by looking at him or her
A girl is grown up when her breasts have come,
A young man when his voice breaks
And hair appears on his face...."[10]

This conscious or unconscious redefinition of the periods of life may explain the intractable problems of child labour and early marriages. The child is called upon early in life to fulfil adult obligations in order to ensure the survival of the group. The best interests of the child are redefined within the context of the best interests of the group. It is therefore no surprise that African governments find it difficult to enforce different conventions and legislations within their largely conservative traditional rural society.

The reticence of sub-Saharan Africa rural communities to change their definition of periods of life, with corresponding social obligations and responsibilities demanded of each period to ensure the survival of the group is largely misunderstood by outsiders and even by urbanised Africans. This reticence is portrayed as being ignorance-based and huge resources are committed to "educate" the people. However, when this "education" is viewed against the background of the implication of the desired change as shown in Chart II above, it is tantamount to "educating" people to accelerate the process of their own extinction. The rural population either reacts by hostility to this attempt or patronisingly humours the advocates of change with feigned acquiescence.

The largely externally inspired and engineered African "government" legislations and the numerous conventions to which these governments readily append their signatures represent a parallel value system to the value system of their environment, which is predicated on the survival of the group in the face of fear and exploitation. These two parallel value-systems can only be bridged when people learn to overcome their fears; and governments learn to provide the right leadership that reduces exploitation to the minimum and inspires confidence and pride in the populace. With the exception of the brief spell of Kwame Nkrumah's visionary period, Sub-Sahara Africa has not been able to put these two conditions together in its history. Rather than tackle the problem head-on through a serious search for home-grown solutions to overcome these fears, Sub-Saharan African leaders have perfected the art of filling the gap between these two parallels with nebulous political rhetoric that are forgotten as soon as they are uttered. These political speeches, devoid of any commitment and many times shallow, only serve to placate and reassure the "International Community" (their own source of fears) of their commitment to maintain the status quo of fears and exploitation in their "countries".

Sub-Sahara Africa is thus faced with a dilemma. If it conforms to universal definitions of lifecycle in its present prostrate form, it faces an imminent extinction, the rate of which will depend on its self-inspired or imposed avidity to blindly embrace non-compatible (with its condition) values. On the other hand, Sub-Sahara Africa cannot isolate itself from useful and scientifically proven universal standards and values in order to have some relevance (not as a yardstick of measurement for all imaginable woes), but as a meaningful contributor to world progress. Sub-Sahara Africa cannot afford to ignore this demand to change from its subservient, prostrate and helpless state into a bold actor on the world stage. Being a subservient and pliable source of raw materials to important economies is not a guarantee that Sub-Sahara Africa will survive; rather it is an ominous indication that when it outlives its usefulness to those who thrive on exploiting it, it will seize to exist. The claim that Sub-Sahara Africa contributes less than one per cent to world economy, despite its reckless squandering of its immense resources should raise an alarm in the minds of all Africans.

The Ultimate
Wages of Fear

The relationship between societies that have somehow overcome basic survival fears and those that live with these fears is a deep-seated, complicated love-hate relationship that has its origins in historical conflicts, religious and ideological divides, economic predation of weak societies by the mighty and powerful, humiliation, and lately, a demand by the powerful, of *master-serf* relationship with the weak societies. Societies that have overcome fears that many others are still grappling with, are very often, consciously or unconsciously oblivious of the enormity of the psychological impact, which their *"we know everything, we own the world, and we dictate to the others"* attitude, has on fear-afflicted societies. This obliviousness or ignorance may have its origins in their erroneous convictions in the ability of handouts or "privileged historical ties" to buy the conscience. These societies tend to be surprised, and are caught unawares when insignificant events tend to flare up deep-seated old prejudices. On the other hand, fear-afflicted societies suffering under the weight of their fears and prejudices also appear not to know what attitude of mutual benefit to adopt with societies that have overcome basic survival fears. Both groups of

societies are at risk for different reasons. We will look at this relationship and the risks, from the point of view of energy dynamics
within, and between the two groups.

The existential dependence of our universe and nature on energy
and its dynamics is a known fact. The behaviour of the elements
and indeed many phenomena of nature have become predictable
because of the understanding of their constituent energy dynamics
and the physical laws that guide them. This understanding has facilitated the simulation of nature and artificial creation of powerful
energy systems.

Energy begets energy. The sustenance of life on our planet is
dependent on the energy from the sun. The planetary sun through a
complicated process becomes the human physiological sun in the
form of adenosine tri-phosphate. The direct link of human existence
to many forms of energy and their different dynamics is a probable
indication that certain physical laws govern the social systems of
structured human society. Under these circumstances, humanity
can then be viewed as an interactive composite system of natural
and man-generated energy. However, unlike some other forms of
energy-systems, the social humanity energy-system is characterised
more by its measurable visible aspect than its invisible but also measurable component. The visible part of the social humanity
energy-system may be interpreted as the different *Value-Added Survival* packages (from the most rudimentary to the most complex)
directed at ensuring the survival of the species and adding to the
quality of life. These packages entail successful acquisition of knowledge to simulate nature, exploitation of nature's resources and a
redefinition of the landscape of nature to contain these advance-
ments. These *Value-Added Survival packages* are exponential energy
gains from comparatively low energy inputs. These gains are visible
and measurable. Their visibility demands that they must have a def-
inite form and shape even if abstract.

Were we to attribute a geometrical shape to this composite energy-system, what interpretable (to an external observer) three-dimensional form would best represent humanity? This form, as a basic rule must be such that it is possible to distribute energy evenly within it, and all parts of it must be visible to an external observer situated at a fixed distance in any direction to it. Moreover, it must be such that a vertical axis passing through the external observer must be equidistant to it. The only geometrical form that seems to satisfy all these criteria is a cylinder. For the purposes of our analysis, we will assume this cylinder to be slim, solid, and elastic to some degree, and we will refer to it as humanity energy pole (HEP).

The analogy of humanity and human development to an energy pole observed at a distance by an external observer may help understand the classification of human societies into so-called developed and underdeveloped. The energy beamed to the observer (located at a fixed distance to the pole) by each component-society of this humanity-pole is the total sum of the exponential energy gains (resourcefulness, innovation, productivity and technological progress) produced by that society. To this stationary observer at a fixed distance, the energy beamed from the top and the bottom of the pole would have to travel at a much greater speed than the energy beamed from the middle of the pole, so that the pole would appear to the observer as straight. If the energy from all points of the pole were to travel at the same speed, then, the pole would appear to be curved (an arc) away from the stationary observer. If however, the energy from either the lower or the upper part of the pole reached the observer before the energy from other parts of the pole, then the pole would appear to slant, either towards or away from the observer.

We are thus faced with the question of what should be the natural state of this humanity-energy pole. Is it a straight vertical pole, a curved one, or a crooked one? Moreover, what factors contribute to its form and shape, and what should be its natural state or form? In addition, we have to answer the question of why some societies of the human race are located at different parts of this pole at a given time. Are these positions on the pole permanent or is there an interchange over a period?

Scholars have proved that there had been a time in human history when all societies were just at about the same level of development. Light beamed from different parts of the pole at that time would have reached an external observer at about the same speed. The humanity-pole was then a curved one.

Newton's first law of motion that "all bodies continue in their state of rest or uniform motion unless compelled by an external force to act otherwise" was the rule, until *internal* changes in some of the component societies compelled them under different guises to act *externally* on other societies, thereby changing the energy distribution between the components of the humanity-pole. These incursive societies overcame fear and took on challenges that changed the nature and the course of history of both the assailant and the assailed. In the case of sub-Sahara Africa, people were not only taken away into slavery, the incursive societies also plundered the resources and remained behind in the name of colonisation to re-engineer the minds of the colonised peoples. Nine hundred years of slavery beginning with the Arabs in the tenth century and ending in the nineteenth century left a colossal damage on the Black African component of the humanity-pole. The energy beamed from this part of the pole gradually lost its speed and the humanity-pole gradually began to straighten out.

Between the sixteenth and nineteenth centuries, some scholars from these incursive societies (consciously or unconsciously) recognising this anomaly attempted to exclude the black race from the humanity-pole. They argued under different guises, using different theories that the black race was not capable of either development or any meaningful contribution to human culture. They conveniently chose to forget the immense contribution of the spoils (both human and material) of their incursion to their own "development".

The man-induced reorganisation of HEP gradually straightened the pole with under-developed societies clustered in the middle and the developed ones at the edges. The energy beamed from the extremes of HEP is much stronger and travel at a faster speed than the energy beamed from the centre. Thus, the pole appears to be straight to the external observer.

With very few exceptions, the symmetry of an entity is a common law of nature. In order to constitute an entity, its components have to arrange themselves in such a way to obey this rule of nature; and in order to function within nature as one entity, the components have to be linked to one another and have to relate with each other. If humanity were one straight pole, what then is its symmetrical part? Where is its symmetrical twin?

If we assumed that "life after death" were the symmetrical twin, then, this would imply that even at the *"heavenly"* level, some groups of people would be at the extreme ends of the pole and some others would be clustered in the middle. In other words, this means that even in *"heaven"*, some groups of people will be, or are more "developed" than others are.

Great and small religions preach equality and justice in "after-life", which in other words mean that light-energy beamed from the different parts of the pole of the "human" population (in whatever form it exists) of heaven should travel at the same speed to the external observer. In this case, the heavenly humanity energy pole is a curved one and therefore cannot be symmetrical in all dimensions to its earthly counterpart. Rather, we will have a D-shaped figure.

If on the other hand, the light beamed from all parts of the humanity pole on earth travelled at the same speed, then the pole would be curved and the curved pole in "heaven" or the "extra-physical" would have found its earthly physical counterpart. Rene Descartes postulated a duality of existence: a physical one and a mental one—the body and the mind. The mind, which is closely identified with the soul in Christian doctrine, is considered immaterial. Since we cannot attribute physical characteristics to this mental existence, we will refer to it in this book as "extra-physical"; however, we will assume that it obeys physical laws. Existence, can therefore be seen either as an ellipse or a circle with a physical half and an "extra-physical" half. Based on this assumption, the humanity energy pole *should be* a curved one and not a straight one as it is today. Energy (which is the total sum of energy produced by the component-societies because of their resourcefulness, innovation and productivity) beamed from all parts of the pole should travel at the same speed towards an external observer.

It is however paradoxical that most religions assuage their oppressed adherents with promises of *"heavenly"* justice. In the same manner, it is also farcical that value-preaching neo-liberals obsessed with exploitative market economy principles source their roots in religious fanaticism. This is a skewed perception that seeks to disequilibrate the natural tendency of life process.

Having concluded that humanity pole *should* be a curved one rather than a straight one (which is the reality of human existence today), we have to answer the question of why and what factors make different groups occupy different parts of the humanity-pole at a given time. In an ideal situation, the position of any society on the pole should not matter much as long as the pole remains curved. However, in a situation of conscious or unconscious man-made stratification of societies resulting in a straight HEP, the analysis of *why and what* becomes pertinent.

The straight, unnatural state of the humanity-pole is characterised by tension within the pole. The state of HEP can be compared to a fractured arm. After a bone of an arm has been confirmed fractured, the doctor sets out to try to put the two ends together in a way to restore the original shape of the bone. He then proceeds to ensure that the two ends stay together (for the healing process to take place) by applying a POP or any other inelastic material to fix the arm in such a position as will not tire the different muscle groups. If the doctor were (for some unknown reasons), to fix the arm along in a straight axis, then all the muscle groups would become tense and the patient would be in pains. The different muscle groups (in seeking to relieve the tension that has built up within them) will twist and turn the arm within its rigid case. Sustained contact of different parts of the arm with the hard case may lead to pressure sores, which may put the whole arm or even the life of the patient in danger. It is the same case when social changes within and between the components of the humanity energy pole force it into an unnatural straight position. Tensions build up. Struggles between the different component-societies of the pole and sometimes intra-component social conflicts arise to restore the humanity-pole to its natural curved state. These inter-component struggles or interactions (sometimes preceded by intra-component social changes) may be expressed in four possible ways.

Firstly, the low-energy cluster in the middle of the pole may exert a centripetal force on the clusters at the extreme of the pole. They seek to pull down the outer clusters of the humanity-pole towards the centre of the pole. It is a way of saying *"if we cannot be like you (and we are not sure we want to be like you), then you have to be like us"*. The centre-clusters may seek to do this through religion, subtle acculturation, or violent extremist activities. The bigger the cluster in the centre, the more the pull on the outer clusters towards the centre of the pole. This pull may come in different forms and from different sources, with the ultimate goal of exhausting the outer components that are, (in order to conserve and protect their way of life and their edge), compelled to engage all their resources (military, financial and ideological) to resist this strong force. To those at the edge of humanity pole, it is a mortal fight for their survival, their way of life and their values; and they will not hesitate to engage the most frightening military hardware to resist this pull. This situation left unchecked and taken to the extremes may mean an end to humanity.

Secondly, large numbers of the members of the centre clusters of the energy pole may seek to migrate or immigrate to outer-cluster societies. They travel in search of knowledge and opportunities, despite the enormous psychological distress that this decision inflicts on them. They weigh one group of fears against the other; and decide that migration or immigration is a lesser fear/evil than their continued stay in their phobia-debilitated, low-energy society of origin. There are some advantages and disadvantages in this tendency. The advantages, when properly managed outweigh the potential disadvantages. These migrations, when properly channelled and managed may serve a long-term purpose of skills acquisition and more importantly, migrants from phobic societies may learn to demystify their fears. The long-term impact and mutual benefit of acquisition of knowledge and skills to dominate fear by migrants, and thus, directly or indirectly influence their phobic societies of origin is lost on the outer cluster societies. The outer-cluster societies consider migration or immigration undesirable because of immediate and medium-term economic costs to them. They believe that migrants want to take advantage of their society and they, having benefited immensely from, and having contributed to the lamentable state of phobic societies of origin of these migrants are reluctant to share even the most insignificant of their spoils with them. Acting on myopic short-term economic and elections-related political point of view, managers of outer-cluster societies devise different means and methods to keep out migrants. They classify would-be immigrants in different categories and *choose* those that satisfy their criteria. They even have different names for their schemes and go to great lengths to advertise these shameful schemes. They choose the best and leave the "undesirables". How can any low-energy society develop and improve itself if there are deliberate schemes by others to haemorrhage its skilled workforce? It is claimed that in the US alone, "African immigrants are the highest educated class in the range of all immigrants....there are over 640'000 African professionals in the US; over 360'000 of them hold PhDs; 120'000 of them (from Nigeria, Ghana, Sudan and Uganda) are medical doctors. The rest are professionals in various fields—from the head of research for the US Space Agency, NASA, to the highest paid material science professors..."[11].

The practice of *immigration choisi* under different pretexts is very reminiscent of slavery, when the odious slave merchants strutted among captives, inspecting them for diseases and their muscle mass and weighing them like sacs before deciding to purchase them. They also chose the best and left the "undesirables".

Free movement of people between clusters may be one of the most effective ways to bridge gaps and restore humanity pole to its natural state. Travel in search of knowledge, opportunities, and to build relationships is a natural human instinct since time immemorial. The fact that some cultures perverted the purpose of travel in recent history should not imply a permanent change or disfigurement of this necessary human desire and instinct. Rather than employ enormous resources to build barriers against human movement and sieving "desirables" from "undesirables", which only serve to create tensions within the humanity energy pole, a more people-friendly approach that will foster friendship between peoples is desirable.

A mutually agreed short-term two-way-migrant-worker exchange presents a possible and just approach to the present humiliating and future problem-generating situation. Under this arrangement, a developed country, X, with a certain number of its citizens working in different sectors of the socio-economic system (multinationals, private companies, Aid, Religion, UN agencies and other sectors) of a "developing" country Y permits a mutually agreed multiple of the total number of its citizens to go and work in this Country X for a non-renewable period of say, two years. With the exception of convicted criminals, under this arrangement, the desirability-factor has to be excluded on both sides.

The question of how to arrive at the multiple-factor number then arises. The multiple-factor number can be calculated using the Per Capita Gross National Income Ratio of the two countries concerned. For example, if the GNI per capita of Country X is 10'000USD and that of Country Y is 200 USD; then the ratio is 1:50. The multiple-factor number can be agreed at say, 20% of 50, which is 10. To illustrate, we will take the example of Nigeria and United Kingdom: In 2005, the World Bank put the GNI per capita of Nigeria at 320 USD and that of United Kingdom at 28'350 USD. This puts the GNI ratio between the two countries at 1: 88. These two countries may reach an agreement that 10% of 88 (8.8) will be the multiple-factor number. Thus, if in a given year, 5'000 Britons are working under, say, a two-year contract in Nigeria in different sectors, (multinationals, private companies, Aid, Religion, UN agencies and other sectors), then the government of Nigeria will have the right, and the government of UK will have the obligation to allow 5'000 X 8.8 (44'000) Nigerians to go to work in UK for a non-renewable two-year period. At the end of two years, this group of Nigerians returns to Nigeria and another group (depending on the per capita GNI ratio) goes to take their place. The economic, cultural, and "development-inducing" advantages of this kind of arrangement are numerous. This arrangement based on measurable indicators like GNI and number of expatriates in a given

African country is a feasible, objective, and monitorable mechanism to bridge gaps between developed and developing nations. It is an effective way to combat human trafficking, brain drain and illegal immigration. The less the difference (or ratio) in GNI between one developed country and a developing one, the less the number of the citizens of the developing country that will be permitted to leave (and certainly, the less the number of people from this developing country who will be interested in leaving their home countries).

Moreover, this arrangement will provide a springboard for real non-aide or debt-tied development. It is a known fact that annual remittances made by Black Africans in diaspora to their home countries far outstrip the total Official Development Assistance funds given to Africa; and more importantly, these remittances reach those in need and make real impact on peoples' lives. In 2005, Africans living abroad remitted a total of about thirty-two billion dollars home. Besides remittances, contacts between Diasporan Africans and their hosts favour commerce, investment, and cultural exchanges. The reverse is also valid for people from other cultures who have come to Africa to work in different capacities. They make even bigger remittances to their home country, and some do go to great lengths to create long-lasting mutually benefiting friendship with some members of their host countries.

The third possibility to restore the natural state of the humanity-pole depends on the outer clusters and is premised on a conscious and honest effort to assist the middle clusters to increase their energy outputs. This may be interpreted as helping the centre clusters to *develop* themselves. The development referred to here transcends a half-hearted, interest-driven, highly mediatised, and intended-not-to-succeed effort. Moreover, it is not a *moral responsibility* as some managers of some of the outer-cluster societies like to claim in their nebulous political discourse. Only the most naïve on all levels of HEP, blinded by their transitory material comfort, and deluded into a false sense of security believe this *morality* argument. The more serious minded see this question as one of the *sine qua non* conditions to ensure the survival of the human species. This "development assistance" should be an unconditional, altruistic all-embracing effort from transfer of technology and technical assistance to actively improving all aspects of social life of the centre clusters. It needs to be delivered in such a way that it can kick-start and accelerate the accumulation of collective energy within these centre clusters. The outer clusters, who have managed to overcome fear and "develop" themselves, should give room to centre clusters to overcome fear and assist them in the process. The Marshall Plan for the development of Europe after the Second World War is a good example of this option. This altruistic approach was not however extended to other cultures neither by the originators of the idea nor their beneficiaries.

Unfortunately, they have constituted themselves into a club of one culture against clubs of *other* cultures. These clubs of *other* cultures are tagged with different identities ranging from religious and ideological to racial, and are all forced through exploitation and manipulation into the centre of the humanity energy pole. The extreme-end clusters (both the saved and their saviours) have through hundreds of years of exploitation, manipulation of others perfected the art of manipulation and exploitation, and any call on their services is analysed under the microscope of *"what do we benefit from this?"* If there are no apparent profits, then the effort is half-hearted and conveyed in such a way that it highlights the helpless dependency of others. However, more often than not, these meagre short-term efforts are structured, planned, and carefully executed by their various institutions as medium and long-term high-yield investments. The *beneficiaries* are called upon to barter their resources for pittances. If the *beneficiary* is history-conscious, he tries to fight off this injustice, but he is soon boxed into a corner of selective sanctions, threats, withdrawal of aid, denial of access to *debilitating* credit facilities. Sometimes, the carpet is taken off his feet along with his shoes though the manipulation of the world price of his cherished resources. The case of Kwame Nkrumah and the deliberate plunging of world price of cocoa in the early 1960s is a good example of this strategy.

Furthermore, the veering-off of the world order in the direction of market economy, which on the long and short term only benefits a few makes this third option a very difficult one.

Conclusively, one can say that the outer clusters, which in a way have it within their powers (through the enormous resources available to them irrespective of their source) to assist the humanity pole to take its natural shape, are, through their myopic obsession with their own interests, inclined to keep the pole in a tense state. This does not augur well for the future of humanity.

The fourth possibility to restore the natural state of humanity energy pole places a responsibility on the centre clusters to individually and collectively organise themselves to produce energy commensurate with the cumulative energy of the outer clusters. This demands a careful review of the causes of their vulnerability and the elaboration of a clear vision. There is dignity in this approach, and it commands the respect of the outer clusters. This should be an all-inclusive, fear-banishing process that makes the best of the potentials of the society, and out-sources necessary skills from the outer clusters. It does not imply copying verbatim what the outer clusters have been able to achieve, neither does it imply seeing oneself through their mirror, it solely involves the generation of useful energy (productive one) that tends to bring the humanity-pole to its natural state. Japan in the immediate post-Second World War period and current China are good examples of this option. The State of Israel with its less than one hundred year of existence is another good example of a society that has successfully employed this option.

Unfortunately, many other members of the centre cluster however have immense difficulties in taking this approach. Many years of exploitation and manipulation by the outer clusters have not only damaged their psyche, but have also sown the seeds of doubts of their own capability in their minds. They fear the known and the unknown; they continue to dread the outer clusters, and have internally generated their own fears, which incapacitate them. Sub-Sahara Africa is a good example of a centre cluster held in the clutches of fear. These low-energy clusters have to reinvent themselves to generate enough energy in the fast changing energy dynamics of HEP, otherwise their band on the spectrum of this energy pole risks being obliterated. In other words, this group faces the risk of extinction in the future. This has indeed happened to some cultures in recent human history, and Sub-Sahara Africa may face the same fate in about five hundred years or less if, nothing is done to reverse the current feeble energy state.

Beloved Africa, "between Alpha and Omega is now; this is the lost time and future time." Heed Seneca: *"Rex est qui metuit nihil"*— "King is he that fears nothing."
Do not let fear kill the baobab.

Endnotes

1. Lenrie Peters—It is time for reckoning Africa. A poem.

2. Wole Soyinka—Interventions I – Bookcraft, Nigeria 2005.

3. Wole Soyinka—Interventions I – Bookcraft, Nigeria 2005.

4. Wole Soyinka—Interventions I – Bookcraft, Nigeria 2005.

5. Julius Nyerere—"Without unity, there is no future for Africa"—New African, February 2006.

6. Abimbola Lagunju. On Development. An Essay. May 2006.

7. Chart: Abimbola Lagunju. . L'Enfance en Afrique. February 2006. Data source: State of World's Children 2005. Unicef Publication.

8. Abimbola Lagunju. L'Enfance en Afrique. February 2006.

9. Abimbola Lagunju. L'Enfance en Afrique. February 2006.

10. Okot p'Bitek: Song of Lawino—East African Educational Publishers 1997.

11. New African August/September 2005.

978-0-595-41370-6
0-595-41370-6